The Bush Theatre and Sheffield Theatres
in association with
Birmingham Repertory Theatre
present

My Romantic History

by D C Jackson

My Romantic History
received its world premiere on 5 August 2010
at the Traverse Theatre

Tour Dates

Thursday 5 August–Sunday 29 August	The Traverse, Edinburgh
Wednesday 1 September–Saturday 11 September	Birmingham Repertory Theatre
Wednesday 15 September–Saturday 2 October	The Crucible Studio, Sheffield
Wednesday 20 October–Saturday 20 November	The Bush Theatre, London

My Romantic History

by D C Jackson

Cast

Amy	Alison O'Donnell
Tom	Iain Robertson
Sasha	Rosalind Sydney

Creative Team

Director	Lyndsey Turner
Designer	Chloe Lamford
Lighting Designer	Philip Gladwell
Sound Designer	Emma Laxton
Graphic Artist	Sean Tidy
Stage Manager	Patricia Davenport
Deputy Stage Manager	Lorna Adamson
Production Manager/ Tour Re-lighter	Daniel Franklin

Set and costumes produced by Sheffield Theatres

Sheffield Theatres and the Bush Theatre would like to thank
Hampstead Theatre, Jo Paul

Sheffield Theatres would like to thank Fellowes

The Bush Theatre would like to give particular thanks to

Company

Alison O'Donnell (Amy)

Theatre for the Bush includes: *Eigengrau*.

Other Theatre includes: *Dolls* (National Theatre of Scotland/Hush Productions); *The Assassination of Paris Hilton* (Racked); *Lady Windermere's Fan* (A Play, A Pie and A Pint); *And The Act Going Home Tonight Is, Skin, Henry's Hangover, Scrabble, Reunion* (DryWrite); *Mad Funny Just* (Creased); *1 in 5* (Hampstead Theatre Daring Pairings); *Phaedre* (Offstage); *Barren* (Old Vic New Voices – The 24 Hour Plays); *The Ghost Sonata* (Goat and Monkey); *Broken Road* (Hush Productions); *Love Sex & Cider* (Jacuzzi Theatre).

Iain Robertson (Tom)

Theatre includes: *The Mysteries, The Winter's Tale, The Good Hope* (National Theatre); *Romeo and Juliet, Blood Wedding* (Citizens Theatre); *The Slab Boys Trilogy, Strangers, Babies* (Traverse Theatre); *Confessions of a Justified Sinner* (Royal Lyceum Theatre); *Strangers Babies* (Traverse Theatre); *Small Craft Warnings* (Arcola Theatre); Lysistrata (Oran Mor).

Film includes: *Plunkett & Macleane, Basic Instinct II, The Debt Collector, The Match, One Last Chance.*

Television includes: *Band of Brothers, Silent Witness, Kavanagh QC, Sea of Souls, Rab C. Nesbitt, Bramwell, Bodyguards, Gunpowder, Treason and Plot.*

Iain was awarded a Scottish Best Performance BAFTA for *Small Faces* and received an Ian Charleson award for Michael Grandage's *The Tempest.*

Iain trained at the Sylvia Young Theatre School.

Rosalind Sydney (Sasha)

Theatre includes: *Pobby and Dingan, Snow Baby, Cyrano* (Catherine Wheels); *Shopping For Shoes, Armchair War* (Visible Fictions); *The Beggar's Opera* (Vanishing Point/Royal Lyceum/Belgrade Coventry); *Subway* (Vanishing Point/Tron/Lyric Hammersmith); *Naked Neighbour, Twitching Blind* (Nick Underwood); *Molly Whuppie* and *Lickety-Leap* (Licketyspit Theatre Co); *We Are Everywhere at Home* (Cumbernauld/Theatro Comedia, Bucharest); *Peep* (Starcatchers); *Zarraberri* and *Limbo* (Oran Mor); *The Littlest Christmas Tree* (MacRobert); *Broken Glass* and *Your Turn to Clean the Stair* (Rapture Theatre Co); *Knives in Hens* and *King Lear* (Tag).

Radio includes: *Raven Black, Meryl The Mounted, Gondwanaland* (BBC Radio 4).

Rosalind trained at RSAMD.

Philip Gladwell (Lighting Designer)

Design credits for the Bush include: *2nd May 1997*.

Other design credits include: *Five Guys Named Moe* (Udderbelly/Theatre Royal Stratford East); *Love The Sinner* (National Theatre); *Nineteen Eighty-Four* and *Macbeth* (Royal Exchange Manchester); *Punk Rock* (Lyric Hammersmith/ Royal Exchange); *Testing The Echo* (Out Of Joint); *Terminus* (Abbey, New York, Australia, Traverse – Fringe First); *Oxford Street & Kebab* (Royal Court); *Amazonia, Ghosts, The Member of the Wedding* & *Fiesta!* (Young Vic); *The Fahrenheit Twins* (Told By An Idiot - UK tour & Barbican); *Low Pay? Don't Pay!* and *Drowning on Dry Land* (Salisbury Playhouse); *I Ought To Be In Pictures* (Manchester Library); *A Christmas Carol* (Dundee Rep); *Origins* (Pentabus); *Daisy Pulls It Off, Blithe Spirit, Black Comedy* & *Dreams from a Summer House.* (Watermill); *Once on this Island* (Birmingham Repertory Theatre/ Nottingham/ Hackney); *Harvest* (UK Tour); *Melody* & *In the Bag* (Traverse); *Aladdin* & *Jack and the Beanstalk* (Hackney Empire); *Mother Courage* (Nottingham Playhouse/ UK tour); *Into the Woods, Macbeth* & *Way Up Stream* (Derby Playhouse); *The Bodies* (Live Theatre Newcastle); *The Morris* (Liverpool Everyman) and *Bread & Butter* (Tricycle).

Opera and dance credits include: *After Dido* (English National Opera); *Awakening & Another America: Fire* (Sadler's Wells); *Il trittico* (Opera Zuid); *Falstaff* (Grange Park Opera); *Canterville Ghost* (Peacock); *Cavalleria, Rusticana* and *Pagliacci* (Haddo House Opera) and the concert performances of Stravinsky's *Violin Concerto*, George Benjamin's *Dance Figures*, Bartok's *Concerto for Orchestra* and Stravinsky's *Oedipus Rex* (Royal Festival Hall).

D C Jackson (Writer)

D. C. Jackson is currently under commission to the Royal Court Theatre and the National Theatre of Scotland and is completing his trilogy for Borderline Theatre with *The Chooky Brae* which tours Scotland in September.

Writing credits include: *Matinee Idle, Drawing Bored, Out On The Wing* and *Company Policy* (A Play, A Pie and A Pint at Oran Mor) and *The Wall* and *The Ducky* (Borderline Theatre).

Chloe Lamford (Designer)

Chloe is winner of the 2007 Theatre Design Award from the TMA for *Small Miracle* (Colchester). Current theatre work includes *Sus* (Young Vic and tour) and *Ghost Story*, a new play by Mark Ravenshill (Sky Arts Live and Riverside Studios).

Design credits include: *Antigone at Hell's Mouth* (Kneehigh Theatre and the National Youth Theatre at the Soho Theatre); *War & Peace* (RSAMD/Scottish Opera); *The Magic Flute* (English Touring Opera); *Kreutzer Sonata* (Gate Theatre); *It Felt Empty* (Arcola Theatre): *This Wide Night* (Soho Theatre for Clean Break); *Good Woman of Sichuan* (New Generation Festival, Birmingham).

Emma Laxton (Sound Designer)

Emma is an Associate Artist at the Bush Theatre and the Associate Sound Designer for *War Horse*.

Design credits for the Bush include: *Like a Fishbone, The Whisky Taster, If There Is I Haven't Found It Yet, 2nd May 1997, Apologia, The Contingency Plan, Wrecks, Broken Space Season, 2000 Feet Away, Tinderbox.*

Design credits for Sheffield Theatres include: *Sisters* (Studio); *The Unthinkable* (Crucible).

Other design credits include: *Travels With My Aunt* (Northampton Royal); *Miss Lilly Gets Boned* (Finborough Theatre); *Off The Endz!* (Royal Court); *Timing* (King's Head); *Ghosts* (ATC, Arcola); *Treasure Island* (Theatre Royal Haymarket); *A Christmas Carol* (Chichester Festival Theatre); *Welcome to Ramallah* (iceandfire); *Pornography* (Birmingham Repertory Theatre/Traverse); *Shoot/Get Treasure/Repeat* (National); *Europe* (Dundee Repertory Theatre/Barbican Pit); *Other Hands* (Soho); *My Dad's a Birdman* (Young Vic); *The Gods Are Not To Blame* (Arcola); *Tusk Tusk, Faces in the Crowd, That Face* (Duke of Yorks); *Gone Too Far! Catch, Scenes From the Back of Beyond, Woman and Scarecrow, The World's Biggest Diamond, Incomplete & Random Acts of Kindness, My Name is Rachel Corrie* (West End/ Minetta Lane, New York/Galway Festival/Edinburgh Festival); *Bone, The Weather, Bear Hug, Terrorism, Food Chain* (Royal Court).

Lyndsey Turner (Director)

Lyndsey is an Associate Director at Sheffield Theatres and London's Gate Theatre.

Directing credits include: *Alice* (Crucible); *Posh, A Miracle, Contractions* (Royal Court); *Nocturnal* (Gate Theatre); *The Lesson* (Arcola Theatre); *Still Breathing, Hymn, What's Their Life Got?* (Theatre 503); *Dealer's Choice* (Central); *The Grace of Mary Traverse* (LAMDA).

The Bush Theatre

'One of the most experienced prospectors of raw talent in Europe'
The Independent

Since its inception in 1972, the Bush Theatre has pursued its singular vision of discovery, risk and entertainment from its home on the corner of Shepherds Bush Green. That vision is valued and embraced by a community of audience and artists radiating out from our distinctive corner of West London across the world. The Bush is a local theatre with an international reputation. From its beginning, the Bush has produced hundreds of groundbreaking premieres, many of them Bush commissions, and hosted guest productions by leading companies and artists from across the world. On any given night, those queuing at the foot of our stairs to take their seats could have travelled from Auckland or popped in from round the corner.

What draws them to the Bush is the promise of a good night out and our proven commitment to launch, from our stage, successive generations of playwrights and artists. Samuel Adamson, David Eldridge, Jonathan Harvey, Catherine Johnson, Tony Kushner, Stephen Poliakoff, Jack Thorne and Victoria Wood (all then unknown) began their careers at the Bush. The unwritten contract between talent and risk is understood by actors who work at the Bush, creating roles in untested new plays. Unique amongst local theatres, the Bush consistently draws actors of the highest reputation and calibre. Joseph Fiennes and Ian Hart recently took leading roles in a first play by an unknown playwright to great critical success. John Simm and Richard Wilson acted in premieres both of which transferred into the West End. The Bush has won over 100 awards, and developed an enviable reputation for touring its acclaimed productions nationally and internationally. Audiences and organisations far beyond our stage profit from the risks we take. The value attached to the Bush by other theatres and by the film and television industries is both significant and considerable. The Bush receives more than 1,000 scripts through the post every year, and reads and responds to them all. This is one small part of a comprehensive playwrights' development programme which nurtures the relationship between writer and director, as well as playwright residencies and commissions.

Everything that we do to develop playwrights focuses them towards a production on our stage or beyond. We have also launched an ambitious new education, training and professional development programme, bushfutures, providing opportunities for different sectors of the community and professionals to access the expertise of Bush playwrights, directors, designers, technicians and actors, and to play an active role in influencing the future development of the theatre and its programme. Last year saw the launch of our new social networking and online publishing website www.bushgreen.org. The site is a great new forum for playwrights and theatre people to meet, share experiences and collaborate.

Through this pioneering work, the Bush will reach and connect with new writers and new audiences, and find new plays to stage.

Josie Rourke, Artistic Director

At the Bush Theatre

We're a full-time staff of eleven, supported by a big team of associates, interns, and freelancers. For ways to get involved, please look at our website www.bushtheatre.co.uk

* **Artistic Director**	Josie Rourke
Executive Director	Angela Bond
Development Director	Trish Wadley
Box Office and Front of House Manager	Annette Butler
Marketing Manager	Sophie Coke-Steel
Producer	Caroline Dyott
Assistant to the Directors	Liz Eddy
Technical Manager	Neil Hobbs
Development Manager	Bethany Ann McDonald
Production Manager	Anthony Newton
Associate Director – bushfutures	Anthea Williams
Assistant Technician	Samuel Charleston
Bookkeeper	Ella Rule
Development Officer	Leonora Twynam
Associateships, Internships and Attachments	
Associate Director	Nathan Curry
Associate Director	Charlotte Gwinner
Pearson Writer in Residence	Nick Payne
Composer on attachment	Michael Bruce
Apprentice	Sade Banks
bushfutures Intern	Lucy McCann
Associate Playwright	Anthony Weigh
Creative Associates	Joe Murphy, Nessah Muthy, Richard Twynam, Ed Viney.
Associate Artists	Tanya Burns, Arthur Darvill, Chloe Emmerson, James Farncombe, Richard Jordan, Emma Laxton, Paul Miller, Lucy Osborne
Box Office Assistants	Kirsty Cox, Alex Hern, Kate McGregor, Ava Jade Morgan, Sade Banks, Karim Morgan, Dervla Toal
Front of House Duty Managers	Sade Banks, Kirsty Cox, Alex Hern, Lucy McCann, Kate McGregor, Ava Jade Morgan, Kirsty Patrick Ward Amanda Ramasawmy, Annie Jenkins
Duty Technicians	Ben Ainsley, Vivienne Clavering, Adam McElderry, Ruth Perrin, Ben Sherratt
Press Representative	Ewan Thomson
Press Assistant	Ava Jade Morgan
Intern	Christina Angus

* **Bold** text indicates full time staff, regular indicates part time/temporary.

The Bush Theatre, Shepherds Bush Green, London W12 8QD
Box Office: 020 8743 5050 | www.bushtheatre.co.uk

The Alternative Theatre Company Ltd. (The Bush Theatre) is a Registered Charity no. 270080

Company registration no. 1221968 | VAT no. 228 3168 73

Be There at the Beginning

The Bush Theatre would like to say a very special 'Thank You' to the following supporters, corporate sponsors and trusts and foundations, whose valuable contributions continue to help us nurture, develop and present some of the brightest new literary stars and theatre artists.

If you are interested in finding out how to be involved, visit the 'Support Us' section of our website, email development@bushtheatre.co.uk or call 020 8743 3584.

Corporate Sponsors
The Agency (London) Ltd
Curtis Brown Group Ltd
Fredereck Sage Co. Ltd.
Harbottle & Lewis LLP
Ludgate Environmental Ltd
Markson Pianos
UBS
West12 Shopping & Leisure Centre

Trusts and Foundations
The Daisy Trust
The D'Oyly Carte Charitable Trust
The Earls Court & Olympia Charitable Trust
The Elizabeth & Gordon Bloor Charitable Foundation
The Eranda Foundation
Garfield Weston Foundation
The Gatsby Charitable Foundation
The Girdlers' Company Charitable Trust
Haberdashers' Benevolent Foundation
The Harold Hyam Wingate Foundation
Jerwood Charitable Foundation
The John Thaw Foundation
The Laurie & Gillian Marsh Charitable Trust
The Leverhulme Trust
The Marina Kleinwort Trust
The Martin Bowley Charitable Trust
Old Possum's Practical Trust
The Peggy Ramsay Foundation
The Peter Wolff Theatre Trust
The Thistle Trust
Split Infinitive Trust
The 2011 Trust

Lone Star
Gianni Alen-Buckley
Michael Alen-Buckley
Christopher Hampton
Catherine Johnson
Caryn Mandabach
Lady Susie Sainsbury

Handful of Stars
Anonymous
Charles Bidwill
Lord Bell
Jim Broadbent
Clyde Cooper
David & Alexandra Emmerson
Chris & Sofia Fenichell
Julia Foster
Douglas Kennedy
Tarek & Diala Khlat
James Lambert
Mark & Sophie Lewisohn
Richard & Elizabeth Phillips
Alan Rickman
John & Tita Shakeshaft
Peter Soros
Mark Tate
Michael Treichl
Ari Zaphiriou-Zarif

Glee Club
Anonymous
John Botrill
David Brooks
Maggie Burrows
Clive Butler
Matthew Byam Shaw
Vivien Goodwin
Simon Johnson
Paul & Cathy Kafka
Neil LaBute
Antonia Lloyd
Michael McCoy
Judith Mellor
David & Anita Miles
Kate Pakenham
Mr & Mrs Alan Radcliffe
Radfin Courier Service
John Reynolds
Barry Serjent
Brian Smith
Nick Starr

The Bush Theatre has the support of the Pearson Playwrights' Scheme, sponsored by The Peggy Ramsay Foundation

---

Sheffield Theatres

Sheffield Theatres is the largest producing theatre complex outside London. With three venues, the Lyceum Theatre, the Crucible Theatre and the Studio Theatre, Sheffield presents a diverse programme of work including drama, dance, comedy, musicals, opera, ballet and children's shows.

In February 2010 the Crucible reopened following a £15 million redevelopment programme. Under the Artistic Directorship of Daniel Evans, the Theatres presented a first season of critically acclaimed, in-house produced work in both the Crucible and the Studio Theatres, including *An Enemy of the People* with Sir Antony Sher, Stephanie Street's *Sisters*, Sam Shepard's *True West*, Laura Wade's *Alice*, a new adaptation of *Alice in Wonderland*, and Polly Stenham's *That Face* with Frances Barber.

My Romantic History is part of the Theatres' second season, and demonstrates its commitment to developing and working with emerging artists. Sheffield Theatres is proud to co-produce *My Romantic History* with The Bush Theatre, opening at Edinburgh's Traverse.

'It is good to have this national asset back.' The Daily Mail

'We love the Studio Theatre. Always a treat.' @faveplaces

Sheffield Theatres Coming Soon

What I Heard About The World

Wed 13 – Sat 30 October   Studio

Remarkable, fascinating, funny and moving tales from across the globe are brought to life by Sheffield's Third Angel and Lisboa's mala voadora.

The Thrill of It All

Fri 15 – Sat 16 October   Lyceum

Acclaimed Sheffield-based Forced Entertainment returns with nine performers to play out a comical and disconcerting vaudeville to the strains of Japanese lounge music.

Beautiful Burnout

Wed 3 – Sat 13 November
Crucible

A Frantic Assembly and National Theatre of Scotland Co-Production

A thrilling new piece of highly physical theatre taking you into the explosively visceral world of boxing.

Age guidance 14+

The David Hare Season

Thu 3 Feb – Sat 5 Mar

Sheffield Theatres presents three of David Hare's finest plays, *Plenty* directed by Thea Sharrock, *Racing Demon* directed by Daniel Evans and *The Breath of Life* directed by Peter Gill.

Support us

Sheffield Theatres is a registered charity. We are proud of our reputation and success, but like all charities, we know that we cannot rely solely on Box Office income and public funding. Whilst keeping our ticket prices accessible, we believe that theatre can inspire audiences and change lives but we cannot do it alone!

Donations from generous individuals, companies and trusts, membership subscriptions and sponsorship have real impact. Monies raised from these sources help us to fulfil our commitment to producing diverse and ambitious new productions of the highest quality and supporting emerging artists and actors, complemented by wide-reaching educational and outreach projects in our region.

The more money we raise from private sources, the more we can achieve.

Contact Leah Woffenden *or* Jess O'Neill on 0114 249 5999

L.Woffenden@sheffieldtheatres.co.uk

J.O'Neill@sheffieldtheatres.co.uk

to find out more.

D. C. Jackson

My Romantic History

ff
faber and faber

First published in 2010
by Faber and Faber Limited
74–77 Great Russell Street
London WC1B 3DA

Typeset by Country Setting, Kingsdown, Kent CT14 8ES
Printed in England by CPI Bookmarque, Croydon, Surrey

A CIP record for this book
is available from the British Library

978-0-571-26957-0

2 4 6 8 10 9 7 5 3 1

Acknowledgements

Josie Rourke, Daniel Evans and everyone
at the Bush and Sheffield Theatres.
Liz Lochhead, Johnny Austin and Kirsty Williams.
Ros, Alison and Iain. Lisa Foster, Dinah Wood
and Steve King. Ben, Edward and Jacqueline Jackson.

The first draft of this play was written while on
attachment to the Royal Court Theatre and was given
a staged reading during the Rough Cuts Season
at the Court in 2007. Substantial thanks are due
to Graham Whybrow, Emily McLaughlin
and Dominic Cooke.

Finally – Lyndsey Turner is my favourite director
and one of my favourite people. Thank you.

D. C. Jackson

Author's Note

I was raised in the fiscally prudent world of Scottish touring theatre so I wrote this play with a cast of three in mind to play all the characters, and that is how it has now been produced.

I see no reason, however, why it couldn't be produced with as many or as few actors as are available to the producer at the time – there's even an argument for more actors than there are characters by double-casting Tom and Amy.

Characters

Tom
Amy
Sasha

Alison
Jessie
Watto
Calvin
Tom's Mum
Tom's Gran
Amy's Mum

Student
Lisa Boyle
Jenny Cooper
Laura Ferguson
Catrina Collins
Craig Bryson
Gary Hay
Cammy Bell
Manuel Pascali
Connor Sammon
Receptionist

MY ROMANTIC HISTORY

This play is dedicated to
the memory of my friend Tom Logan
who was taken before his time
in the period between writing
the play and the production.

D. C. Jackson

Act One

SCENE ONE

Tom *Where do you meet people? Where are people meeting each other? Pubs? The gym? The supermarket? Fuck off.*

Where are people meeting each other? I'll tell you where.

If you haven't met someone by the time you graduate, you're going to marry some cunt from your work. I'm not shitting you. It's that simple. Do you know how they get animals to breed in captivity? They put them in the same cage.

Sasha Hi, Thomas? I'm Sasha. Really good to meet you.

Tom And you.

Sasha So . . . I'm going to show you around and sort of get you orientated and stuff.

Tom Great.

Sasha This is your office. I'll get you your email address sorted out this afternoon and your number is written on the phone.

Tom Great.

Sasha Nine for an outside line. I'll show you where the tea and coffee and stuff is.

Tom Great.

Sasha The building's a bit of a labyrinth.

Tom . . . Great.

I always come across as a tit when I'm trying to make a good impression – 'GREAT'!

Sasha Okay . . . so I'll just leave you to it. But give me a shout if you, you know, you need anything. Or whatever.

Tom Okay.

The first week is always the longest. I just keep my head down and say as little as possible.

Sasha Hi, Tom.

Tom Sasha!

Sasha So, how's your first week been?

Tom Fine. It's fine. Work's work. You know. Everyone seems really . . . nice and . . . everything.

Sasha We're all going for a drink tonight after work if you'd like to join us.

Tom Yeah, that sounds . . .

It sounds shit. I hate all that. Bonding. Colleagues. Bonding with colleagues.

SCENE TWO

Amy You're Thomas, aren't you? I work on the second floor. I'm Amy.

Tom Amy? Hi.

Amy So how are you finding it?

Tom It's okay. I don't know, I mean, it's fine, it's great.

Amy It's always horrible, isn't it? Starting a new job?

Tom Yeah.

Amy Och – it isn't that bad. I've worked much worse places.

Tom Me too. I've worked in call centres. Honestly, it's fine. I'm quite enjoying it.

I can't have just one drink. Can you? Can anyone? When have you ever gone for 'a' drink? It's nine or none.

Nine drinks later – the brown mist has descended and Amy and I are back at hers. We don't go to mine because it smells of bins and my sheets are rank – I say I don't have any central heating. In Glasgow that's like saying you don't have an inside toilet.

Amy What would you like to drink?

Tom Whatever. Anything. I don't mind.

Amy Sweetheart Stout?

Tom That's fine.

Amy I'm joking.

Tom Sorry, I'm a bit pissed.

Amy Me too . . .
I like your hair . . .

(*She lunges at him and they kiss awkwardly.*)

Tom *So it's the next morning.*

Amy Morning.

Tom Morning.

(*She tries to kiss him. He pulls away.*)

Amy What's wrong?

Tom *Alison Hamilton. Alison Hamilton. Honest to God, I still get a partial semi just saying her name. Alison Hamilton.*

Alison Fuck off. Loser.

Tom *That was what it was like at the beginning. She couldn't stand me. I was a year younger than her. And of course that mattered.*

Alison Stop staring at me.

Tom *We got the same school bus and I used to just sit and gaze at the back of her head. It had erotic contours.*

Alison Stop looking at me.

Tom Sorry.

Alison You freak.

Look. I don't like you. I don't fancy you. I will never get off with you. I will never be your girlfriend.
I will never be your friend.

Tom *She did become my friend though. In fifth year I was in her Modern Studies class.*

Alison I can't believe my Modern Studies class is so full of wankers.

Tom *I was the best of a bad lot.*

Alison You're the best of a bad lot.

Tom *Eventually she even sat with me on the bus. But then she got her licence halfway through her sixth year and I ended up alone again, staring at the lumpy, misshapen back of Muir Mair's head. Counting the dandruff. Then one Friday she offered me a lift –*

Alison Do you want a lift home?

Tom Well. Em. Alright. I mean. Em. Yeah. That would be good.

I was actually meant to be going to my gran's house. She would understand though. She was always asking me why I didn't have a girlfriend.

Gran You still no got a girlfriend, son?

Tom No.

Gran Aw. Never you mind, pet. There's plenty of time.

Tom *Those ten-minute car journeys home were probably the happiest I've ever been. Even now the smell of a Magic Tree gives me the horn. Peep-peep.*

What are you doing at the weekend?

Alison Julie's having a party.

Tom I heard that.

Alison Are you going?

Tom Maybe, I don't know . . .

Alison Were you invited?

Tom I . . . em . . . no.

Alison Which one is your house again?

Tom It's the small one with the overgrown garden.

Alison Well. Here we are. See you on Monday.

Tom Yeah. See you.

Alison Have you done something different with your hair?

Tom No – I washed it last night though.

Alison It looks good. You should keep washing it.

Tom Thanks. I will.

Alison Well . . .

(*He tries to kiss her.*)

What are you doing? Jesus Christ, Tom.

Tom Sorry . . . I thought.

Alison Well, don't. It would take more than some shampoo. You can get the bus on Monday.

Tom *So I feel a bit shitty. Because I'm not a monster.*

Amy What's wrong?

Tom Nothing. I mean. God. God, I was drunk last night.

Amy Right.

Tom No, I don't mean, I mean . . . Look. It's not that.

Amy Not what?

Look, it's fine. Don't worry about it.

Tom Please, I'm not trying to be all . . . cuntish or whatever. It's just that we – You know.

Amy Had sex?

Tom And don't get me wrong – I enjoyed it. It was . . . great. Really. Smashing. But I mean . . . we work together. I've just started. It's awkward. It isn't a good idea . . . you know.

(*He kisses her goodbye.*)

Thanks for everything. Really.

And I'm off into the morning. Last night's clothes, death breath and my hands stinking of my new colleague Amy's twat. Don Juan in Denniston.

SCENE THREE

Tom *Bit awkward at work on Monday. You know. Embarrassing. I understand the psychology of the sex killer. We all do. If we're honest. Men. See the appeal of hacking them to pieces and putting them in bin-bags afterwards.*

You know, because at least then you'd be sure you'd seen the back of them . . .

Sasha Did you have fun on Friday?

Tom On Friday?

Sasha After work. We went for drinks . . .

Tom Oh right, right. Yeah, it was good.

Sasha You and Amy seemed to get on well.

Tom Eh. Em. I mean. Yeah. She's nice. Everyone's really nice.

Get up to anything at the weekend?

Sasha I go to a samba-drumming class on Sunday.

Tom Oh right. Samba-drumming?

Sasha Yeah. It's really good. Well. I mean. If you like that kind of thing.

Tom *Who likes that kind of thing? Is there even a kind of thing? I suppose there is. Capoeira. Yoga. All that bullshit. God, I hate white people.*

Great.

Sasha We're doing a performance. Next week in George Square. You should come. If you're not – You know. Doing anything else.

Tom *Why would I want to go and see her samba-drum? Samba-drumming is more intrusive than road works. Bam-bada-bada-badamp-pam-pum.*

It sounds really good. But I don't know what I'm doing next week – I've got a thing that . . . I mean I sometimes . . . I think that I might have something on so . . .

Sasha Sure – no pressure. Do you want a coffee or anything? I'm going to the kitchen.

Tom Nah, I'm alright thanks. I've already had three. I'm at maximum coffee velocity.

Sasha Okay. See you later.

Tom Yeah. See you.

Amy Hey, you.

Tom Oh. Em. Hey, Amy. How are you?

Amy I'm fine.

Tom Good.

Amy How are you?

Tom Good.

Amy Good.

Tom Good.

Well. This is awkward. And here it comes –

Amy Listen. Maybe we should talk about the other night.

Tom Right. It's a bit. Em. I mean I'm a bit. Just now . . .

Amy I don't mean right now.

Tom Of course. Sure. Brilliant.

Amy So do you want to maybe go for a drink or something after work?

Tom Um. Em. I mean . . .

May as well get it over with. No point in dragging it out.

Yes, sure.

Amy Do you want to go home first?

Tom After work is fine.

Amy Great. Well. See you later.

Tom *Oh my God. Am I in a relationship? I spend the afternoon forensically replaying everything I've ever done to her, and her to me. Attempting to establish my obligations.*

Amy Hey, mister.

Tom Oh, hey.

Amy So . . . how was work?

Tom Yeah, it was fine. You know.
Slogging away at the coalface . . . Pushing the envelope . . .
Shifting some paradigms.

Amy Yeah.

Tom *So* . . .

Amy The photocopier is pretty shit, isn't it?

Tom Em. Yeah, I suppose.

Amy You haven't used it yet, have you?

Tom No, no I have. The one on the third floor?

Amy Yeah.

Tom Yeah, I mean, I suppose it is a bit shit. I don't know that I'd recognise a good one.

Amy The laminator is worse.

Tom Right. I don't think I'll have much need to laminate.

Amy No. I don't really either. But laminating is sort of exciting.

Tom But the laminator's shit?

Amy Yes.

Tom I had fun the other night. It was. Em.

Amy Smashing?

Tom God, did I say that? Sorry. I can be a prick sometimes.

Amy Yeah.

Tom Yeah. Anyway. I had fun.

Fun. That's a universally understood code, isn't it? Fun.

Amy So did I. That's why I thought it would be good to get a drink. You know. Away from work and everything. And em. Talk.

Tom Yeah.

What about? I said I had 'fun', isn't that the conversation over? I had 'fun', you had 'fun', let's never do it again.

Amy I don't know about you but I was pretty pissed on Friday.

Tom Yeah, me too.

Amy So. You know. We shouldn't expect anything.

Tom No. Sure. You're right.

Amy So let's just see where it goes.

Tom *Why does it need to 'go' anywhere? I don't think it should. I think it should just stay where it is.*

Stay. Stay. Staaaaaay.

Amy What are you having?

Tom Em. Another Guinness, please.

A big disadvantage of sleeping with colleagues is that they pretty much know your schedule, so you can't cry off with the vague, all encompassing 'work' get-out. You know –

'This was great but I need to go – I'm up early for work / I've got a work thing to finish tonight / I'm expecting a call for work.'

So we end up sleeping together again, because at the time it seems easier to than not. And as she said, no one expects anything. So it's a freebie.

SCENE FOUR

Sasha Will I see you on Sunday?

Tom On Sunday?

Sasha The concert thing.

Tom Oh right, yeah, I dunno.

Sasha It's fine, it's fine – absolutely don't worry about it.

Tom No, no, I mean I'd really like to see you drum, really. /

Sasha No, no, it's fine, honestly –

Tom / Really. I would. What time are you on?

Sasha It starts at twelve.

Tom Are you on first?

Sasha No I think we're like seventh or something.

Tom *Seventh? Good God, how many samba bands are there in Glasgow?*

What time does it finish?

Sasha Three, I think. I think it's about three.

Tom I'll hopefully get down.

Sasha Cool, well no worries, I mean . . . it's no stress if you don't make it. I'll see you, Tom.

Tom See you.

Sasha Bye.

Tom *First Amy, now Sasha. I'm like catnip to the women of this office.*

The older a man gets the more attractive he becomes. And that's not just Clooney and Connery and cunts like that. It's true what they say – all the good ones are taken. And once that happens the average ones become the good ones and the bad ones become the average ones. Eventually I bet even Schmek from my school will be upgraded to marriage material. And he used to eat glue and wank in maths.

I'm a B. A solid, dependable, not-too-flashy, not-too-shabby B. At school I was a C. Minus.

In the Easter holidays of 1996 Jerry Richmond had a party in which five fish and a guinea pig – Axl, Izzy, Steven, Duff, Slash and Sparkle – died, two windows and Robert Jelly's nose were broken and a TV and video, a decorative hookah pipe and every Richmond family photo album was stolen. He had an attractive sister.

Also – I finally got off with Alison Hamilton.

Alison Where's Chris?

Tom He went home.

Alison Where's Chris?

Tom He went home.

Alison No. Chris went home? But it's still early.

Tom It's five o'clock in the morning. Are you okay?

Alison I'm having fun. Are you having fun?

Tom Yes.

Alison You're more fun away from school.

Tom Thanks.

Alison Because I always thought you were a dick.

Tom Oh. Right.

Alison But you're more fun away from school.

Tom Thanks.

Alison Where's Chris?

Tom He went home.

Alison Do you want to get off with me?

Tom *And once the seal was broken . . . we spent memorable months together.*

Before she left for Canadian Camp America.

I wish you weren't going to Canada.

Alison Oh, shut up.

Tom I'm going to miss you so much.

Alison I'm only going for the summer.

Tom The whole summer.

Alison I'll be back.

Tom In September.

Alison You can write me letters.

Tom *The summer draaaaaagged.*
Then I'm talking to my best friend Jessie outside the Mason's Apron. Jessie's a boy, by the way, and he's pretty shirty about it – like the boy named Sue.

Jessie So which one do you want?

Tom I just miss her.

Jessie Out of sight, out of mind.
What one do you want? Michelle or Fat Rhoda?

Tom Alison. I just miss Alison.

Jessie I understand. I get it. Listen – how long's she doing Canadian Camp America for?

Tom All summer. God it's *so* long. I miss her *so* much.

Jessie Yeah. I know, buddy. So. Who do you want?

Tom What?

Jessie Michelle or Fat Rhoda? I'll take Rhoda if you want, I don't mind . . .

Tom I don't want either of them. I just want Alison.

Jessie Did she tell you anything? Before she left?

Tom She told me she loved me.

Jessie Apart from that.

Tom That she'd write every day.

Jessie And has she?

Tom No, but it's hard because –

Jessie And that's it? That's all she told you?

Tom What do you mean?

What is it? You're starting to freak me out here.

Jessie She was cheating on you.

Tom WHAT?

Wait for it. This is fucking priceless.

Jessie With Mr Wood.

Tom This is a joke.

Jessie No joke.

Tom The music teacher?

Jessie Look, I'm really sorry, I didn't think it was my place, but –

Tom – Mr Wood? Mr Wood? Mr *fucking* Wood?

Jessie Yeah.

Tom Are you sure?

Jessie Yeah.

Tom But he's a fucking dick.

Jessie Yeah, it's like it says in the girls' toilet, but ay no? Mr Wood would.
Honestly, mate – you take Michelle – I don't actually mind going with big Rhoda.

Tom *I never liked Mr Wood. He chewed gum and thought he was a bit cool and even though I was only sixteen I could see he was a sleazy loser. He was thirty-odd, for fuck's sake. Big man with the sixth-form girls. Dick. I'm not sure we called them paedos back then, but I'd call him a paedo now. Paedo.*

Alison.

Alison What? Who is this?

Tom 'S Thomas. Alison. 'S Thomas.

Alison I can't talk now. I'm working. I can't believe you said it was an emergency.

Tom *Is* an emergency. *Is* an emergency. Alison . . .

Alison What?

Tom Alison.

Alison *What?* What is it? I need to go.

Tom Alison . . .

Alison Call me when you're sober.

Tom Mr Wood? *Mr fucking fucking Mr Wood.*

Alison Oh.

Tom *She wasn't that receptive to my attempts at a drunken heart-to-heart. She had left a game of spelling softball unsupervised.*

So that was that. We were broke up and I was desolate. Desolate.

So, you know, pardon me if I'm not in a hurry to break out the Milk Tray and flowers and rush back into all . . . that again. Because where does it get you? Monomaniacal devotion? And it's one thing when you're a gangly teen shooting spunk out of you like a water pistol . . . but a man needs to keep his options. You know. Open.

Amy I saw you talking to Sasha earlier.

Tom *It's like I'm under fucking surveillance. Is she compiling a dossier on me? For HR?*

Oh right. Yeah. Yeah, I was talking to Sasha. Earlier.

Amy Are you being weird?

Tom No.

Cool your jets, Clutchy McMan-Trap.

Amy Okay . . .

What was she saying to it?

Tom Who?

Amy Sasha . . .

Tom Right. I don't know. Something about samba-drumming.

Amy Typical. That's typical Sasha. I hate samba-drumming. She's such a hippy.

Tom Yeah.

Amy She used to wear a *bindi*. You know. One of those Indian spots.

Tom God, I bet she did. Fucking hippies.

(*She kisses him.*)

Not at work.

Amy No one's about.

(*She playfully lands another on him. He recoils.*)

Tom I know. But not at work.

Amy God. When did you become Mr Conscientious?

Tom It's just – I don't know. Inappropriate.

Amy Inappropriate – fuck off.

Tom I'll see you later on.

Amy Bye.

Tom *So it seems like she's my girlfriend. And I didn't mean for that to happen. It's kind of like I went to the presentation to get the Marks and Spencer's vouchers and somehow I ended up with a time-share in Crete. Still. I haven't met a girl yet I couldn't make chuck me. I'm like a romantic Gandhi. Passive resistance.*

I put her on the programme –

No proactive phone calls or texts. No weeknight dates.

I maintain a Saturday-evening obliga-date. Pictures, then hers.

I establish a generally shitty attitude which I employ at every opportunity. Because as I understand it – that's how the Indians got rid of the Raj.

Amy Do you want anything to eat?

Tom Em.

Amy Do you want anything to eat?

Tom Yeah, I heard you. I dunno. What have you got?

Amy What do you want? I have a kitchen full of food, do you want me to list everything? Is there something you feel like?

Tom Oh, I don't know. It's fine.

Amy Do you want a sand

Do you want a sandwich?

Tom No, it's fine. Honestly. I'm fine.

Amy I've got some chilli from earlier. I could make you some rice.

Tom It's cool.

Amy You said you were hungry.

Tom Yeah. I'm okay now.

Amy Do you want a drink?

Tom I suppose. Can I put the TV on?

Amy What's on?

Tom Does it matter?

Amy The remote is on the table.

Tom *I don't even like football. I have no idea who these teams are. Is this English football? I'm supporting the purples. Come on, you purples!*

Amy Here.

Tom Cheers.

Amy Football?

Tom I can switch it off if you want.

Amy No. It's fine.

Tom *This is one girl one time. And I'm not dumping her. I'm letting her dump me. Which is kinder.*

Mum You're not leaving school.

Tom I'm leaving school.

Mum You're not leaving school.

Tom I am. I'm going to university.

Mum What are you going to study?

Tom Theology. Theology or Land Economy.

Mum Why?

Tom That's all I can get in to at Dundee.

Mum Dundee? Why do you want to go to Dundee?

Tom I've always wanted to go to Dundee.

Alison was going to Dundee.

Mum Why?

Tom I don't know. The jute.

Alison was going to Dundee.

Mum You've never even been to Dundee.

Tom Exactly.

Alison was going to Dundee.

Mum I know what this is about. Girls don't want you following them. Chasing them. Crowding them.

Tom *This one isn't getting any choice. I have never been more certain of anything in my life . . .*

Mum It'll get easier. The first cut is the deepest. She isn't worth it. There are plenty more fish in the sea. You're too young to be so serious. Time is a great healer.

Tom *. . . If I can just be there. With her. She'll want me again. Maybe not immediately, but eventually. We are destined to be together.*

I'm fine. There's nothing wrong with me.

Mum Oh, Tom . . .

Tom *Dundee is a shithole. Seriously. It's worse than Aberdeen.*

Alison Thomas. What are you doing here?

Tom Studying.

Alison What?

Tom Studying. I'm doing a BTh.

Alison What's a BTh?

Tom A Bachelor of Theology. I'm going to be a minister.

That'll show her. She's driven me to religion. I look like I'm so heartbroken I'm devoting my whole life to God. That's going to work. That's a grand romantic gesture. She's going to be putty in my hands. Chicks dig vicars, right?

Alison Right. Great. Thomas, look. Look, Thomas. You know nothing's going to – This is crazy. I'm sorry. Look.
I don't want you –

Tom But –

Alison – I've moved on. This is what happens. People move on. They change. They grow.

Tom Grow?

Alison There's someone else.

Tom Mr Wood, I know . . .

Alison Not Alan.

Tom *Alan. Alan. I'm not even making this up.*

Alison I'm with someone else now.

Tom Who?

Alison Does that matter?

Tom I want to know.

Alison Steve.

Tom Who's Steve?

Alison You wouldn't know him. We're in the same hall of residence.

Tom *Except I did know him. It was Steve who used to go out with Jessie's big sister Rachel. That Steve gets to fuck everyone. She was right. It was over. He was in his twenties, for God's sake. That's how grand romantic gestures end. Sleazy Steve from school nut deep in the love of your life.*

SCENE FIVE

Tom *It's lonely in bed with some girl. If that's all she is. You know. Some girl. I like Amy. I do. But it's not love, it's not anything.*

I'm awake and it's too early to leave without making it a thing. The purples lost. Last night. Typical. Our chat's running out – she's in reruns already. I'm hungry.

I've got a massive erection. Like every Sunday.

Explain that, Dawkins.

She's asleep.

She's definitely asleep.

(*Tom slowly begins to masturbate. Carefully checking Amy is still asleep at appropriate intervals. Eventually he becomes too engrossed and doesn't notice her waking.*)

Amy WHAT THE FUCK ARE YOU DOING?

Tom Nothing. Morning.
Sorry. I didn't mean . . .

Amy CHRIST.

Tom I wasn't doing anything . . . Sorry.

Amy?

Amy It's okay. Morning.

Tom Sorry. I wasn't. I'm sorry.

Amy Just a bit. Christ. Morning.

Tom Morning.

That's got to be a black mark, surely? I don't know a lot about women but I'm pretty sure they frown on you wanking in their bed. She's going to have to chuck me.

Amy Jesus.

Did you sleep well?

Tom Not really.

Amy What was wrong?

Tom Ah, nothing. It's fine.

Amy Bad dreams?

Tom It's fine. I should . . .
I need to get up.

What is it going to take to end this fucking thing?

I've got things to do.

Amy Like what? It's Sunday.

Tom I know.

Amy So? What do you have to do on a Sunday?

Tom I don't know. Jeeso – why does it even matter? Just stuff.

Amy I thought we could spend the day together. I'll come with you.

Tom No, don't. It's easier if I do it alone.

Amy God, you're being so mysterious. Are you buying me a surprise present?

Tom Yeah. Big present.

(*He gets up.*)

Amy Are you leaving right now?

Tom *That's the good thing about staying over at hers. If she'd stayed at mine I would have had a nightmare shifting her. Honest to God, I feel like I've been conscripted. Conscripted into the Amy. Whoa whoa, you're in the Amy now. Well, I'm a conscientious objector. I choose to refuse the draft. I head to George Square which in this metaphor serves as the Canadian border.*

Sasha Hi. You made it.

Tom Well, I –

(*Loud noises of samba-drums deafen them. They valiantly attempt to converse but are totally drowned out. Once it finishes they pause to make sure the drumming has stopped before:*)

Sasha I'm really glad you –

(*The drumming starts again, then stops.*)

I'm really glad you made it.

Tom Yeah. Well. I mean. Samba-drumming.

Sasha Isn't it?

Tom Yeah.

It really really is.

I thought I would have missed your set, to be honest.

I thought I would have missed her set, to be honest.

Sasha No, everyone's running long.

Tom Really?

Sasha Yeah. We're on next.

Tom Right.

Sasha So . . . I'd better go.

Tom Right. Sure.
Are you about afterwards for a drink? Or . . .

Sasha Oh, sorry, Tom. We're all going on to a barbecue thing afterwards.

Tom Oh, okay . . .

Sasha I mean, you'd be totally welcome to come, but you can't. It's at someone's house . . . so . . . you know . . .

Some other time.

Tom *Is that a raincheck or a brush-off?*

SCENE SIX

Tom *A relationship can be habit-forming. It's nice eating breakfast, for instance. I don't mean with her. She's kind of intrusive and irritating and never gives it a rest in the mornings. But she makes me breakfast. And she drives me to work. Door to door. If I was left to my own devices I'd still be having a cigarette and a big cough. She makes me smoothies. And muesli. It's like being in a concentration camp run by Lorraine Kelly.*

Amy What are we doing tonight?

(*He ignores her.*)

What are we doing tonight?

Tom *God, she is persistent. She's like the fucking Terminator.*

Amy What are we doing tonight?

Tom I don't know. I kind of wanted to spend the night at my flat.

Amy Okay.

Tom Okay?

Amy Yeah, that's fine.

Tom Oh. Right. I kind of thought you'd kick off.

Amy Don't be silly.

Tom Okay. See you later.

Amy What time?

Tom Sorry?

Amy What time should I come over?

Tom What?

Amy What time should I come over to your flat?

Tom Oh, right. I kind of meant that I would stay there. Just I.

Amy Oh.

Tom I just need to do some stuff and I thought. You know. It might be nice to have a bit of 'Me-time'. Do you mind?

Amy No . . . no. It's fine. Honestly.

Tom Sometimes it's good to be alone for a bit.

Amy 'Me-time' I understand.

Tom Great.

See you later on.

Amy Yeah. See you.

Tom Hey, Sasha. How are you?

Sasha Hey, hey . . . Not bad. Not bad. Did you enjoy the concert?

Tom The concert?

Sasha Thanks for coming. I told everyone and you're like the only person from work who came.

Tom Don't mention it.

Sasha Well. I'd better get back to my desk.

Tom Yeah. Sasha . . .

Sasha What?

Tom Are you doing anything tonight?

Sasha Just my washing.

Tom Quick drink after work?

The easiest way to end a relationship, and the most final way, is just to start fooling around with someone else. She'll be a bit pissed off, sure, but at least it's over. For good. The will-o'-the-wisp of love has moved on and it will not be denied. That's why we forgave Brad and Angelina –

Alison Hi, Thomas.

Tom Alison! How are you? What are you doing here?

Alison This is where my mum and dad live. What are you doing here?

Tom Em. I was. I was. Em. Just passing.

Alison Where were you going?

Tom Em. Just for a walk.

Alison So what are you doing now?

Tom Nothing much. You heard I dropped out? Just chilling. How about you?

Alison I'm just home for the holidays. See the folks. That kind of thing.

Tom How's second year going?

Alison Fine.

Tom How's Steve?

Alison Steve?

Tom Yeah, Steve, you know, *Steve.*

Alison Steve. Right. We broke up –

Tom I'm sorry.

Alison – a while ago.

Tom Oh, right.

Alison I've got a new boyfriend now, though.

Tom Right. Anyone I know?

Alison Em. It's Watto.

Tom Watto? Ian Watson?

Alison Yeah.

Tom No way!

Christ, she doesn't spread her net very wide, does she? Scotland has a population of five million and she has to go out with my music teacher, my best friend's big sister's boyfriend and Ian fucking Watson.

Ian Watson was the rhythm guitarist of my band at school. I was the lead singer. She was being deliberately perverse. You don't go from the lead singer to the rhythm guitarist. I never liked Ian Watson. Smug prick. He was only in The Twisted Biscuits because he had a garage we could practise in and a big Marshall amp. Well, he won't be playing at the reunion tour, I can tell you that.

Right. That's . . . nice.

Alison I'm going in.

Tom Well, good to see you.

Alison Are you just going to stand there, then?

Tom Are you asking me in?

Alison I'm asking you not to stand in my garden.

Tom Oh. Right.

A day or so later I bumped into Ian Watson outside the baker's. I was halfway through a pasty and my chin was glistening with mutton grease from the pie I'd just finished. I'm a big baked-savoury enthusiast.

Watto Alison was saying you'd been to see her.

Tom No, I was just going for a walk. Bumped into her. Nice to see her and everything, you know, but I was just out for a walk.

Watto Baws.

Tom What?

Watto Baws you were. You were stalking her. You're a fucking stalker, Thomas.

Tom Fuck off.

Watto Just stay away from Alison. She doesn't want anything to do with you.

Tom Says you.

Watto That's right, motherfucker. Says me. Her boyfriend.

Tom Just now.

Watto When was the last time you were? 1996? Do yourself a favour, Tom. You look pathetic.

Tom You look pathetic.

Watto Dry your eyes, wipe the grease off your chin and get over it.

Tom Quick drink after work?

Sasha Look, Tom. I don't think that would be a good idea. I'm kind of seeing someone right now.

Tom *Fuck. Fucking. Fuck.*

Sure. I understand.

FUCK. Fuck. I'm such a fucking idiot. I tried to pull the Sashachute and it failed to open. I stew for a bit then rally. Fundamentally that was just one option.

Plan B – just stop answering my phone. Might not work. She's got my direct line and you know she could probably just pop a note in my pigeonhole if worst came to worst . . .

Plan C – say my ex and I are going to give it another go. Always strong, hard to argue with.

Plan D – suggest a ménage.

And then suddenly it seems like my luck's changing because the next day this happens. Amy goes . . .

Amy We need to talk.

Tom *There's only one thing that means. I'm telling you, man, passive resistance is the shit. I submissed her into submission.*

Free at last. Free at last. Thank Lord God Almighty, I am free at last.

Amy I'm pregnant.

Tom *And everything's fucked.*

Act Two

SCENE ONE

Amy *I suppose there comes a point when you have to face that you're just 'that age' and that if you've got a man who isn't a retard, a rapist or a Rangers supporter then he's probably about the best you're going to get.*

Mum Amy, do you remember Geoff Davies?

Amy Em. I don't know.

Mum You do. You remember my friend Geoff. He gave you a Christmas present last year.

Amy Oh right, yeah – the vouchers. I should do something about them. What about him?

Mum So you do remember him?

Amy Yes.

Mum We're getting married.

Amy Oh.

Apparently they've been going out since August 2007 and he seems okay. I mean, it's not like he's going to be my new dad, I'm hardly ever home and she's going to keep her name so . . . good luck to them. He seems like a pretty good guy and he must make her happy. I don't know. It doesn't seem like a great love or anything but she's obviously decided he's the one . . .

My mum's 'that age'. The giving up and settling age. I'm not . . . in case you thought. Christ. I'm only thirty-three.

It's still on my mind at work on Monday, though.

Sasha There's a new guy on the fourth floor.

Amy Oh right.

Sasha He's the new Charlie.

Amy What's he called?

Sasha Tom.

Amy Right.

Sasha Yeah . . . he seems cool.

Amy Really?

Sasha Yeah, kind of. No – he is. He is. I really think you might dig him.

Amy Dig him?

Alright, Cilla. Davina. Holly fucking Willoughby.

Sasha Yeah. I think he might be your type. Sorry. That's really annoying, isn't it?

Amy Yes.

Sasha I can't believe you're still single though. You know. I mean what chance do the rest of us have?

Amy I thought you were seeing someone.

Sasha Well, I mean, I am right now but – You know.

Amy *So I'm compelled to go to the fourth floor on spurious business. Just to see. I mean, Sasha wants to fuck off. Obviously. Can you imagine? What she thinks my type is. Some drooling halftard.*

Hi, is Charlie about?

Tom I'm the new Charlie. I'm Tom.

Amy Oh. It doesn't matter. Thanks.

Fail. He looks like a gimp. Of course he does. Thanks, Sasha. A dishevelled nerdy gimp.

Of course you can't tell though, can you? That's the thing about boys. Men. Boys. All you can tell by looking at them is what they look like. And what does that tell you? Nothing at all because some of the best don't look it.

Calvin Kennedy. That was his name. Mixed marriage.

Calvin Hey, Amy – wait up.

Amy Em . . .

Calvin You saw that, didn't you?

Amy What?

Calvin The face he pulled when he got me to do that reading.

Amy Em . . . no . . .

Calvin Yes you did, you saw it. Revelation 22:15.

And how come I had to collect in the hymn books? Again?

Amy What are you talking about?

Calvin Father Terry is pure always discriminating against me.

Amy How is that discriminating against you? Discriminating about what?

Calvin Because he knows I'm a half-caste.

Amy What?

Calvin I'm not a Fenian.

Amy But you go to a Catholic school. That makes you Catholic. It goes by what school you go to. That's why Martin Clarkston chucks stones at our bus.

Calvin I'm just here undercover. My dad's a pure big mad Tim and he thinks me and my brother are too. But we urnae.

Amy You're not?

Calvin No way. Martin Luther, John Knox and Ally McCoist are my guys. I'm subverting the system from within. Just you wait. I'm going to bring it to its knees.

Amy What?

Calvin The Roman Catholic Church.

Amy If you bring it to its knees it'll just have a big old pray.

Calvin Seriously, man – fuck the Pope and the IRA. I'm going to destroy the Vatican. Starting with St Francis's Secondary.

Amy You're weird, Calvin Kennedy.

Calvin Yeah.

Amy *Not that I'm saying new Charlie is a Calvin Kennedy. Trust me, he isn't. He's barely even the new Charlie. It's pretty pitiful to say – because I'm thirty-three now – but Calvin Kennedy is still the love of my life.*

SCENE TWO

Amy *We go for drinks after work on a Friday. Sometimes it isn't actually hideous, if I've got nothing better . . . else to do. Socialising with colleagues, though . . . it's only one step up from posting on internet message boards or something. It offers a kind of facsimile of real human contact, but it . . . it's just bullshit.*

You're Thomas, aren't you? I work on the second floor. I'm Amy.

Tom Amy? Hi.

Amy So how are you finding it?

Tom It's okay. I don't know, I mean, it's fine, it's great.

Amy It's always horrible, isn't it? Starting a new job?

Tom The people seem . . . *nice* though.

Amy *It's coming on to me. I am ashamed to admit that I'm flattered. I remind myself that I didn't have anything to eat during the day – so the wine went to my head. Which I'd like to say is unusual.*

And then, after they call last orders and we're all heading out the door, he puts his hand on my back, like guiding me out. And we both know.

Tom Listen, we'll need to go to yours because I don't have any central heating.

Amy *I prefer to go to mine. When boys take you home it's like being given a guided tour of the shittest museum in Scotland. They have this bizarre compulsion to show you things, give you a tour of their stuff –*

Tom This is my collection of Japanese . . .

Amy *It's always some Japanese thing.*

Tom This is my collection of . . . Japanese horror comics –

Japanese cooking knives –

Vintage Japanese Nikes . . .

Oh wait, wait, you've got to listen to this song, this song is *awesome*!

Amy *And they never have anything good to drink. Beer. Water. Something from holiday. I'm a grown-up – you know? I have options.*

What would you like to drink?

Tom Em . . . Anything. I don't mind.

Amy Sweetheart Stout?

Tom That's fine.

Amy *He doesn't care.*

I'm joking.

Tom Sorry, I'm a bit pissed.

Amy Me too.

Tom You're really sexy.

(*He lunges at her and they kiss awkwardly.*)

Amy *So it's the next morning. I wake first. He looks different in daylight. Worse. I can smell him from the other side of the bed. Which is where he is. The far side. He smells like bums.*

Morning.

Tom Morning.

Amy *I can barely remember what we did last night. After we got to bed. I'll still have to wash the sheets, though, won't I? And they were clean on yesterday.*

There was some kissing and I don't have my knickers on. Oh God, now he thinks I'm interfering with myself. I go to kiss him.

He's embarrassed about his breath. He should be. His mouth smells like Bobby Sands' prison blanket.

What's wrong?

Tom Nothing. I mean. God. God, I was drunk last night.

Amy Right.

Tom No, I don't mean, I mean . . . Look. It's not that.

Amy Not what?

Look it's fine. Don't worry about it.

Tom Please, I'm not trying to be all . . . cuntish or whatever. It's just that we – You know.

Amy Had sex?

Tom And don't get me wrong – it was . . . smashing. But we work together. I've just started. If this goes sour then –

Amy 'If this goes sour'!? If what goes sour? I was pretty drunk too but I don't think we got married, did we?

Tom Oh God. Look. Sorry. I'm sorry.

Amy I think you should leave.

Yet another Amy MacIlvanney sexual success story . . .
Calvin Kennedy got expelled from school for arguing with the priest and writing unionist graffiti in the boys' toilets. Mark Joe Kelly said it was for sucking off the janitor, but that wouldn't make any sense. How come the janitor kept his job? Well . . . fucking Catholics . . . But Mark Joe Kelly talks out his arse. He used to say his uncle was Steven Seagal.
He wasn't. Once we were at different schools there was an urgency to our affair. Calvin insisted we use condoms.

Calvin One in the eye for the Pope.

Amy Is this a good idea?

Calvin I think so.

Amy Me too.

Calvin Good. Then it is.

Amy And you're not going to be – You know. Weird after?

Calvin No. Well. No weirder.

Amy *And he wasn't. He held me tight like I was being washed away and for a moment I felt like I'd grown up.*

Calvin Amy.

Amy What?

Calvin You know I love you.

Amy I love you.

Calvin But I mean. Really. Really. I really really love you.

Amy I know. Me too.

Calvin We can never break up.

Amy Never.

Calvin Never.

Amy *Being young is so fucking easy.*

SCENE THREE

Sasha I've been watching *The Wire* on my laptop.

Amy Is your telly broken?

Sasha No, God . . . I don't have a TV, because it's all, like, so rubbish, isn't it? But *The Wire* is *amazing*, isn't it? It's like Dickens or Zola or something.

Amy Yeah . . .

She doesn't have a TV. Doesn't that tell you everything you need to know? And she thinks that makes her in some way morally or intellectually superior. Fucking pesto-munchers, man. Dickens would have had a telly. Zola would have had a telly. Zola would have fucking loved telly.

Sasha Hey. So . . . what happened with you and Tom?

Amy What? Oh nothing.

Sasha That's what he said. You're so boring.

Amy Sorry about that.

Sasha Hey. Hey. Come on. You'll meet someone soon. I can just tell.

Amy *Fuck. Yoooooo.*

That's what some girls are like. Passive-aggressive boots. It's brutal. Makes you almost appreciate men. And she just assumes nothing is happening. We left the pub together. We were both pissed. He had his arm on my back. So what? I'm like some incompetent-crap-lay? Or frigid? Or incapable? Fuck yoooooo, Sasha.

Hey.

Tom Hey, Amy.

Amy How are you?

Tom I'm alright.

You?

Amy Yeah, I'm fine.

Tom Cool . . .

Amy *Is this how it's going to be now?*

And I can feel fucking Sasha judging me a fannyless incompo-pump . . .

Listen – do you want to maybe go for a drink or something after work and, em, talk.

Tom Um. Em. I mean . . . yes, sure.

Amy Do you want to go home first or . . .

Tom After work is fine.

Amy Great. Well. See you later.

See, Sasha? Do you see? Not only did we do it on Friday, now we're dating. Like fucking Americans. Fuck yoooooo.

Tom Oh, hey.

Amy So . . . How was work?

Tom Yeah, it was fine. You know.

Amy Slogging away at the coalface . . . Pushing the envelope . . .
Shifting some paradigms.

Tom Yeah.

Amy *So as you can see, it's all going rather badly.*

Tom I had fun the other night.

Amy Oh? Em, me too.

Before I booted him out like a mental.

Tom Yeah. It was. Em.

Amy Smashing?

Tom God, did I say that? Sorry. I'm a prick sometimes.

Amy Yeah.

Tom Anyway. I had fun.

Amy Me too. But Friday night was Friday night. And you know . . .

I don't want to get myself married off to this just to get it up Sasha.

So can we just . . . start again?

Tom Sure.

Amy *But I feel like I may as well give him a chance – he's seen my weird birthmark now.*

Two drinks later and I think I'm starting to get to know him. The real him. Not Tom from work. Tom.

Tom Yeah, I played badminton at quite a high level. They wanted me to go pro but, you know, it's only really worth it if you're Lin Dan or Eddy Choong or one of those guys and I'd probably have just been, like, an ordinary pro on the tour, well not ordinary but . . . blah blah blah, blah blah, badminton, blah blah, blah blah blah, that's when my parents moved house, blah blah blah, isn't even a bedroom in the new place for me, blah blah, sewing room, blah blah, Alison Hamilton, blah blah blah, pretty serious about my music back then, blah. Blah. BLAH.

Amy *He comes back to my flat without an invite and I can't be bothered making it an issue. Drunk on a school night. And once he's there . . .*

SCENE FOUR

Amy *Still, that'll give Sasha something to shut-the-fuck-up about.*

What was Sasha saying to it?

Tom When?

Amy When you were talking to her.

Tom Oh right. Yeah. Yeah, I was talking to Sasha. Earlier. Em. I suppose I was. Talking to Sasha.

Amy Are you being weird?

Tom No, no . . .
No, I'm not being weird.

Amy Okay . . .
What was she saying to it?

Tom Who?

Amy Sasha . . .

Tom When? Right – sorry. I don't know. Something about samba-drumming.

Amy Typical. That's typical Sasha. I hate samba-drumming. She's such a hippy.

Tom Yeah.

Amy She used to wear a *bindi*.

Tom A what?

Amy You know. One of those Indian spots.

Tom A paki dot!

Amy What?
WHAT?

Tom Sorry. Sometimes that kind of thing slips out. Sorry. A *bindi*.

Amy That's not cool.

Tom I know. I'm not being racist.

Amy Well, you are.

Tom I'm not *a* racist then. Sorry.

Amy Okay . . .

Tom It's just what we used to say, at school. I've practised saying the 'corner shop' and the 'Chinese restaurant' and everything, but it just . . .

Amy *I kiss him just to make him stop talking.*

Tom Not at work.

Amy No one's about.

Tom I know. But not at work.

Amy God. When did you become Captain Conscientious?

Tom It's just – I don't know. Inappropriate. I'll see you later.

Amy Yeah. See you later.

My man – he's vague and evasive and probably racist. What. A. Catch. I give the whole disastrous project a week tops before the minor thrill of proving a point is dwarfed by the major tedium of Tom.

Calvin was unbelievably, totally, devoted. I realise he sounds like I'm making him up, like he's 'a boy from holiday' or something. But I'm not and he wasn't. He really loved me.

Calvin Sometimes when I'm at school –

Amy At your proddy school.

Calvin – at my non-denominational school.

Amy Who does your religious instruction?

Calvin There almost isn't any. They don't care about our souls.

Amy . . . When you have it?

Calvin Ministers.

Amy Proddy ministers at your Proddy school.

Calvin So? Are you going to let me finish?

Amy Sorry.

Calvin Sometimes when I'm at school, I think about things.

Amy What things?

Calvin Us. You. Me. I mean. It's. These things, they don't last.

Amy Are you breaking up with me?

Calvin No. No, that's not it. I mean, these things, they never last. And I can't. Amy. I can't cope with that.

Amy What do you mean?

Calvin I'd rather die than not be with you, Amy.

Amy You're with me.

Calvin Because I am always going to love you, Amy. And we're going to be together even when we leave school and you go to college and become a lady barrister and I become a counter-revolutionary paramilitary.

Amy Where's your dad?

Calvin Pigeons.

Amy What time is your mum back?

Calvin Late. It's her line-dancing.

Amy Do you want to do it?

Calvin Line-dance?

Amy No.

Calvin Yes.

Amy *Sex with Calvin Kennedy.*
What he lacked in technique he made up for in enthusiasm. His rabid anti-Catholicism made him an adventurous, committed and considerate lover.
Sex is like everything. It all gets older as you do. Becomes familiar. Rote. Boring.

SCENE FIVE

Amy *Tom came to pick me up on Saturday night and he was wearing his one nice shirt. He had made himself a little hairstyle with some product in it and he had on a jacket. He looked pretty sweet.*

Hey.

Tom Hey. You ready?

Amy Em. Nearly.

Tom Is the cinema alright?

Amy It's fine.

Tom Is there anything you want to see?

Amy Don't mind.

Tom *Professor Hat*?

Amy I suppose. It's a bit –

Tom *Shit Storm*?

Amy Have you seen *Floral Bonnet*?

Tom No.

Amy Do you want to?

Tom I suppose. That's fine.

Amy Really?

Tom Yeah. Honestly. I don't mind that stuff.

Amy You big softy.

Tom I'm quite hungry. Have you eaten?

Amy Yeah. There's some left, I could heat it up for you.

Tom Nah, it's alright. I'll just get something out.

Amy You sure?

Tom Yeah.

Amy It's chilli.

Tom It's fine.

Hey.

Amy Hey.

We necked in the pictures like a pair of horny teens. Came home. Hung out. Went to bed.

I love Sundays. They're usually spent smoking weed and watching teen dramas and eating ready meals. But it makes a nice change. Not being alone on a Sunday morning. When you wake up. That feeling of an occupied bed . . .

(*Tom is masturbating.*)

What the fuck are you doing?

Tom Morning.

Amy *He's wanking.*

Stop it. FUCK.

Tom Sorry. I didn't mean . . .

Amy CHRIST.

He's wanking.

Tom I didn't mean to . . . Sorry.

Amy?

Amy *He's wanking. Jesus. What the fuck? Maybe he wasn't. Maybe I'm still half asleep. Maybe he was still asleep.*

It's okay. Sorry. Morning. Sorry.

Tom No. I wasn't wanking. I mean. I'm sorry.

Amy *He was wanking.*

Just a bit. Christ – Morning.

Tom Morning.

I should. I'd better. I need to get up. I've got things to do.

Amy It's Sunday.

Tom I know.

Amy *He's fleeing the scene of the crime. I wonder how long I need to continue this charade to get the message to Sasha. I'm capable – I'm normal, I date, I'm not some sad case who can't get a fucking man.*

Are you leaving right now?

Tom Do you mind if I take a toilet roll? I haven't got any I don't think.

Amy *We never stay at his. Not that I want to. But that creates a real, tangible, mathematical inequality. Because if we both start out with one whole flat and I share part of mine with him but he keeps all his to himself that means what? He gets a flat and, like, a third and I only get a fraction of a flat? That isn't fair. It's uneven. Unequitable. He has somewhere to go and 'recharge' and I get to stay here and tidy everything for him to mess it all up again. I know that I sound really petty but he's taking away toilet paper now. Expensive foo-foo toilet paper. What a prick.*

Tom So it's okay? To nick a bog roll? Thanks. I'll text you.

Amy *What am I doing? Jesus Christ. I think we're about done here. Tom and I and our half-baked romance.*

(*Amy is sick. She composes herself.*)

Calvin and me kept going out even though we were at different universities. Our love sustained on late-night phone calls, letters, awkward visits . . . and then I started cheating. They appreciated my kind of beauty more at university. I got distracted.

Calvin It's great to see you. I've missed you.

Amy Em. Me too.

Calvin You don't sound very convincing.

Amy No, I did, I did.

Calvin I really missed you, Amy. I mean really. I *really* missed you.

Amy Calvin . . .

Calvin Amy?

Amy Calvin . . .

Calvin What is it?

Amy We need to talk.

Calvin Oh God no. No, Amy, no.

Amy You don't even know what I'm going to say.

Calvin Yes I do. People only say 'We need to talk' when the next sentence is 'We should break up'. They never say 'We need to talk . . . about the implausibility of transubstantiation . . . about what we can do to achieve social justice . . . about our favourite film moments . . .' Oh fuck it.
  Why, Amy? Why? I love you so much.

Amy We're just in different places right now.

Calvin Edinburgh is only forty minutes away from Glasgow, Amy.

Amy In our lives.

Calvin No, we aren't. We're in the same place – university. We're just in different cities. I'll transfer. I'll drop out. I'll make it work. Please don't, Amy, please . . .

Amy *But I did.*

SCENE SIX

Amy *If it hadn't been for university maybe Calvin and I would still be together. A long-distance boyfriend is like an imaginary friend – at the very least they need to be present. Tom's got that going on. He's relentlessly present. He's here. There. Everywhere. I see him at the tea and coffee area.*

Tom Hi.

Amy *In the canny.*

Tom Hi.

Amy *By the photocopier.*

Tom Hi.

Amy Hi!

Tom Hi, Amy. Listen. I kind of wanted to spend the night at my flat. Is that okay?

Amy Okay.

I still haven't been to his flat. But of course that day was always coming. It's grimly inevitable. And once the Pandora's box is open . . . I'll have to stay over in it. All the time. And what if he's got a guitar? And he plays it? And I have to pull my 'I'm-listening-to-you-play-the-guitar' face.

If he was less here, there and everywhere I could just take the night off.

Tom Okay?

Amy *G–o–d . . .*

Yeah, that's fine.

Tom Oh. Right. I kind of thought you'd kick off.

Amy Don't be silly.

Tom Okay. See you later.

Amy What time?

Tom Sorry?

Amy What time should I come over?

He's going to cook me his 'speciality'. And it will be shit. It's always shit. Some crappy risotto or something.

Tom What?

Amy What time should I come over to your flat?

Tom Oh, right. I kind of meant that I would stay there. Just I.

Amy Oh.

Oh.

Tom I just need to do some stuff and I thought. You know. It might be nice to have a bit of 'me-time'. Do you mind?

Amy No . . . no.

No. My Sky-Plus is teeming with unwatched episodes of Shag Valley *and I can drink white wine and get stoned on my own. It's like a mini mini-break.*

It's fine. Honestly.

Tom Sometimes it's good to be alone for a bit.

Amy 'Me-time' I understand.

Tom Great.

See you later on.

Amy Yeah. See you later on.

When you first meet them they're all so upright and . . . independent. They all have their own wallets and keys and they buy you drinks and open doors and book restaurants and . . . play the part. After about a month you realise they're holding your hand crossing the road, you're not holding theirs . . . and you have to make them their fucking breakfast in the morning just to shut them up and get them out your fucking flat.

I'm not really a morning person.

Calvin visited me again the next weekend. Unannounced. And as luck would have it I was alone.

Calvin Amy. You and me.

Amy Calvin . . .

Calvin Don't say anything.

Amy Calvin . . .

Calvin Just let me speak. I've got to get it all out in one – er . . .

Amy Beat.

Calvin I fucking love you, Amy. I mean. *I fucking love you.* You know?

Amy I . . .

Calvin Don't. I've done something.

Amy What?

(*Calvin reveals a tattoo that reads* 'AMY MACILVANNEY' *in huge gothic calligraphy on his back.*)

Oh my God.

Calvin Let me finish.

Amy You got a tattoo.

Calvin Let me finish.

Amy You got a tattoo.

Calvin Let me finish.

Amy You got a tattoo.

Calvin I'm not mental, Amy. I know you want to break up. I understand. I do. It's a break-up tattoo.

Amy A break-up tattoo?

Calvin You made me. I mean it. You're the cauldron in which I was forged. I love you. I know it's over, but I fucking loved you for real and I want to remember how you made me feel for the rest of my life.

Amy I don't know what to say . . .

And can you blame me? What the fuck do you say to that?

SCENE SEVEN

Amy *The boy I had been sleeping with in halls left me soon after Calvin's body-art exhibition – for a boring, flat-chested medical student called Jayne. They're married now. And I cried myself to sleep for the rest of the term. Thinking about him and about Calvin and about that stupid big tattoo.*

I was at university and drinking my own weight in home-brewed wine. It was called the Solomon Grundy Seven Day Wine Kit, and the slogan was 'Brewed on Monday, drunk by Sunday'. It tasted so bad we used to add Kia-Ora. Which honestly improved it. Three pints of Solomon Grundy and Kia-Ora would make anyone emotional. Luckily this was the days before mobile phones and the perils of drunk dialling. But you know. You can stand in a queue for the payphone in halls and dial drunkly pretty effectively if you have a mind to.

Student Hello?

Amy Is Calvin Kennedy there?

Student Who?

Amy Calvin Kennedy.

Student What room's he in?

Amy 42A.

Student Hold on.

Amy *Remember this shit? Changed days. Mobile technology. Bet they're Skyping each other on their iPads now.*

Calvin Hello?

Amy Calvin.

Calvin Amy. Do you know what time it is?

Amy I'm a bit drunk.

Calvin Amy . . . this isn't right.

Amy I just. I just –

Calvin Amy, we'll never be apart. Never really. We're soulmates. You and me. But we talked about this. We talked about the perfect ending.

Amy Maybe we could . . . have a sequel.

Calvin Sequels are never as good.

Amy *Empire Strikes Back.*

Calvin Exception which proves the rule.

Amy *Godfather Part Two.*

Calvin Amy.

Amy There's someone else, isn't there?

Calvin Yeah.

Amy How does she feel about the tattoo?

Calvin She doesn't love it.

Amy *Poor cow. Poor bastard . . .*
Poor me . . . Poor Tom.
Tom.
I mean there isn't necessarily anything better. At least he likes me. At least he's here, now. But how do you know? It's like a big, horrible, endless game of Deal or No Deal.
And I always said if I was on Deal or No Deal *I'd just say –*
'Stop fucking about, Noel – I want Box 11.'

Sasha Hey, Amy.

Amy Sasha.

Sasha Do you have a tampon or a towel or something? I use a mooncup but I don't have it with me and I've come on.

Amy A mooncup?

Sasha Yeah I got it at Glastonbury. You should get one – it's changed my life.

Amy What is it, like a hemp Tampax or something?

Sasha It's a menstrual cup. You know. Greener. I mean, think how many trees we use, just for . . . that.

Amy *I haven't been on for . . . three, four . . .*

Sasha But it's actually really comfortable too. You only need to empty it like three times once it's in.

Amy *Six, shit, it'll be seven weeks on Monday . . .*

Sasha It doesn't leak or smell or anything. It's great.

Amy *Jesus Christ. I'm fucking pregnant. I'm fucking pregnant. I'm fucking fucking pregnant.*

Sasha But I don't have it with me – brought my gym bag, so . . . do you have anything?

Amy Uh-huh . . .

I am thirty-three years of age. I have never been less married. I have a job, friends, and a flat stuffed with bullshit I bought, but I am completely, totally, profoundly alone. I immediately think about a girl I saw struggling to get her buggy on the bus this morning. It draws everything into clear focus.

Tom.

What Tom is for.

Tom.

We need to talk.

Act Three

SCENE ONE

Tom *I've always liked kids. A lot. And I want babies of my own. But that's the problem. I want babies of my own. And you don't get them. You have to share them with someone you've slept with. And quite frankly I'd be more inclined to share an STD with most of the girls I've slept with than a baby.*

Your parents and school and stuff, they go on and on and on about how hard it is having a baby. Well, that's bollocks.

Forcing a girl to have an abortion against her will? Now that's hard.

Amy I haven't decided.

Tom You know that I'll support whatever you decide.

Amy Really?

Tom Believe me. I'm not one of 'those guys'.

Amy I'm sorry.

Tom Hey. Come on. It's not your fault. It's both our fault. I mean. It isn't anyone's fault. It doesn't have to be terrible.

Amy It'll change both our lives for ever.

Tom If we keep it.

Amy Well. Yes.

Tom Is that what you're thinking?

Amy I don't know.

Tom You know I'll stand by you. Financially.

Amy What do you mean, 'financially'?

Tom What do you mean?

Amy Why did you say 'financially'?

Tom Look. We need to talk about this. About us.

Amy WHAT?

Tom Don't freak out. But look, Amy. We've only been seeing each other for a month or something.

Amy I'm pregnant.

Tom Exactly. I know. But look. If you decide to keep it then I'll be there for you in every way I can.

Amy So . . .

Tom But we can't stay together.

Amy What?

Tom If you keep the baby we can't stay together.

Amy Why?

Tom It isn't fair.

Amy On who?

Tom On any of us. You. Me. But most importantly it isn't fair on the baby.

Amy What?

Tom It won't last. We'll end up hating each other. Is that what you want? Both unhappy? At each other's throat. I'm not trying to be a cunt here. I really like you, Amy. A lot. But we need to be grown-up about this. This matters.

Amy So what if I had an abortion?

Tom That would be different.

SCENE TWO

Amy *What happened? What was that all about – all the flirting and kissing and compromising and his little hairstyle and his suit jacket and . . . everything? That was the point of him – he loved me enough to make up for . . . Christ. He doesn't. He loves me not. I have been so stupid.*
Motherfucker.

It's like a fucking tsunami up inside here. It's like Sky News in my brain. The ticker is scrolling.
I'm having a baby. An abortion. A baby. An abortion. I can't have both.

Hello? Mum – it's me.

Mum Hello, darling.

Amy How are things?

Mum Fine – listen, darling, can I give you a ring back? Geoff's just cooking me dinner and he's making a huge mess!

(*Geoff and Mum are laughing.*)

Amy Yeah . . . that's fine . . . It's just that –

Mum Thanks, darling. Speak soon.

Amy – I'm pregnant.

SCENE THREE

Tom *What did she think? What did she think I was going to say? Brilliant? Terrific? Fucking smashing? 'I better phone my folks'?*

'Mum, Mum, I'm going to have a baby . . . with some cunt from my work . . . Yeah . . . like I'd always hoped . . . Yeah, complete accident, path of least resistance, inertia, yeah.'

She's back at work the next day. Makes me feel like a prize shit. Because, you know, it isn't even just her – I have a mental list of people she might have spoken to. Told. I have to consult it every time I leave my desk. Plan my route. Keep my head down. Fag breaks. Stationery refills.

So I eat my lunch in the disabled toilet. I always fancied having sex in here but this is okay too.

You can use the baby-changing area like a picnic table.

Friday drinks are a pain in the hoop – my absence will be noted. By Joyce and Gillian and Sasha and all those bitches. I go for gimpy drinks at the other pub with the guys from my department. Conor Sammon dominates the conversation. He's an alpha male.

Conor Sammon I'm an alpha male.

Tom Really, Conor? An alpha male . . .

Conor Sammon Yup. It's because I have an undescended superfluous third testicle.

Tom *I drink up, make my excuses and leave. Conor Sammon is lifting his shirt and presenting an unusual lump in his abdomen as I go.*

I am making sacrifices.

I'm not oblivious. Or evil. Or . . .

I want the best for Amy. I want the best for everyone. I buy a shit kebab on my way home. It's shit. I nearly call her but I don't.

SCENE FOUR

Amy *I throw down at Friday drinks. Might as well. Enjoy myself. Not staying pregnant. So . . . And it turns out I have absolutely no single friends left. So . . . go team!*

Sasha Whoa – hey, Amy. You're really putting them away.

Amy Yeah.

Sasha Are you okay?

How is everything?

Amy?

Amy I'm fine, thanks. Everything's fine. How are you?

Sasha Brilliant. Really brilliant.

Amy Great.

Sasha Yeah. Everything is going so well. It couldn't be any better really. I'm moving in with my man.

Amy You're moving in with your –?
Oh, God, sorry, Sasha. I just always thought. Sorry. Nothing. That's great.

Sasha No, no . . . what did you think?

Amy Just that. This is embarrassing. I always thought you were gay!

I know she's straight. Fuck yooooo, Sasha.

Sasha Wow. No. I mean. You know.

Amy So what's he like?

Sasha He's great. He's from my samba-drumming class. He's called –

Amy Samba-drumming? Great! Samba-drumming . . . He's a samba-drummer . . . Sasha and the samba-drummer . . .

Sasha We're doing a concert next month. You should come.

Amy That sounds . . .

Shit, it sounds shit.

Sasha So . . . what's going on with you?

Amy *If you ask me again I'm going to tell you. And that'll shut you up. I have access to conversational plutonium.*

Sasha Amy? Are you okay?

Amy No. I'm thirty-three and everyone else is married. My mum's getting married, my sister is married – even my gay friend Helen is married, civil married, gay married – whatever, and . . .
  And . . .

Tick tick tick . . .

And I'm pregnant.

BOOOOOM!

Sasha Wow.

Amy *Now the aftershock –*

With Tom's baby. And he's effectively. Forcing me to. You know.

Fuuuuck. What have I done?

Jesus. Forget I said all of that. Please? I'm just a little bit tipsy.

Sasha Fuck, Amy. That's heavy. What are you going to do?

Amy Getting rid.

Sasha Are you sure?

Amy Sure I'm sure. Listen – seriously, can you just forget all that. I'm a bit tipsy . . .

SCENE FIVE

(*Amy is being sick.*)

Amy *Really bad hangover the next day. The worst maybe of all time. It hurts to move so I don't. It hurts to breathe. But I have to.*

It's pretty pitiful that Sasha from work is the only person I can talk to – tell – talk to. But she was kind. Really. She's okay. Really. Nice. She's arranged everything for me. Like it's just another stationery requisition. Which is . . . but it's . . . nice. And she said she'll come with me . . .

I just don't want to go alone.

Tom is absent. Nowhere to be seen. It must take an effort – being that invisible. We work in the same building, with the same people, at the same time. I'm not having the termination because he told me to. Fuck him. I'd rather he stayed invisible. It's just that it's more time wasted – some more of me wasted. On someone else who could never love me a half as much as Calvin Kennedy.

Calvin I hope you are pregnant, Amy. I really hope you are. I want us to make babies. And even if you're not now, we will. I'm going to father your children.

Amy *That's what you're meant to say. Someone should tell them that. They should have a man-manual.*
Calvin Kennedy . . . And his big tattoo.

Calvin It's a break-up tattoo.

Amy *And he was only a boy then and the men since . . .*
Craig Bryson –

Craig Bryson I got you something.

Amy *He got me a teddy holding a love heart with a teddy in the middle of it holding another love heart with a little tiny teddy embroidered in the middle of it holding a minuscule love heart. Gary Hay –*

Gary Hay Happy Valentine's Day, sexy girl.
I made you a quiche.

Amy *Cammy Bell. Cammy Bell was the first person to ever give me flowers –*

Cammy Bell They're plastic. So they'll last for ever.

Amy *Manuel Pascali – he was Italian.*

Manuel Pascali For you, bella Amy.

Amy But –

Manuel Pascali Shhh, it's nothing, baby.

Amy Bu—

Manuel Pascali Shhhh.

Amy B—

Manuel Pascali Shhhhh.

Amy But I don't smoke.

Manuel Pascali Oh, sheet. Right right right – wrong Amy.

Amy *Conor Sammon –*

Conor Sammon I got you a vibrating dildo.

Amy *I'm like the Statue of Liberty. Sexually. Give me your tired, your poor, Your huddled masses yearning to breathe free, the wretched refuse of your teeming shores . . . All that.*

It's pitiful. I meet man after man. They never last. No one can love me like I need to be loved. Like Calvin. There's some kind of fundamental dislocation. My heart is buried in the 1990s. I may as well give up. Because here I am. Thirty-three. Almost halfway done. Alone.

Except suddenly it hits me – I'm not. Am I? Alone? I'm not alone. It's like Stockholm syndrome – children's love, parents. Objectively my dad is a complete prick but I still love him.

'I love you, Mummy.'

I can call it Calvin.

SCENE SIX

Tom *Even though I'm right, and what I said was right, and it's for the best I feel guilty. Shitty. Low.*

I wonder how she is. Because I'm a good person, I wonder how she is. Because I do care. I wonder how she is.

Sasha You're a piece of shit, Tom.

Tom Sasha?

Sasha You're a complete arsehole. You're pathetic. I can't even fucking look at you.

Tom Is this about the microwave? Because I don't use it. It isn't me. I don't even eat soup.

Sasha It isn't about the fucking microwave, Tom.

Tom Oh. Right.

I can't believe she told Sasha. She must have told everybody.

Listen, Sasha. It's complicated.
I mean. I know how it looks.

Sasha It looks like you're a total shitbag.

Tom But nothing's one-sided.

I'm the victim. Really. If you tally one column up against the other. I mean. Working backwards. Lisa Boyle –

Lisa Boyle I want to go out with someone else.

Tom Who?

Lisa Boyle I don't know yet. Just someone else.

Tom *Jenny Cooper –*

Jenny Cooper I don't love myself or anything. I hope this doesn't sound arrogant, but there are seven billion people in the world. So – there's like three and a half billion men? I just feel like with those odds I can probably do better.

Tom *Laura Ferguson –*

Laura Ferguson You actually make me feel physically sick, Tom. You give me the creeps.

Tom *Catrina Collins.*

Catrina Collins I'm getting married.

Tom Who to?

Catrina Collins Jason.

Tom Your brother Jason?

Catrina Collins He's my stepbrother.

Tom *And that brings us to Alison Hamilton. Alison fucking Hamilton . . .*

SCENE SEVEN

Amy So I need the number of the place. Because I'm not going to be doing that now. So I should cancel the appointment.

Sasha Okay. Wow. Is this because of –

Amy What?

Sasha No. Nothing.

Amy Say what you were going to say, Sasha.

Sasha Has Tom changed his mind?

Amy No. It's got nothing to do with Tom. *Nothing.* I'm going to just have it on my own, just me and it, just the two of us.

Like Sarah Connor and John.

Tom isn't involved.

Sasha God. What a rotter.

Amy A rotter?

Sasha You know. A dick.

Amy I don't even blame him, Sasha. He's just collateral damage. Friendly fire.

Sasha Good for you.

Amy I blame the condom machine in the Vanity Bar.

Condom-machine condoms are like a fucking placebo.

Sasha You're going to be fine, you know, Amy. Amazing. You're going to be amazing. You're so strong.
I think it's just wonderful.

Amy I mean. Something had to change some time.

Sasha You're going to have a baby! You're so lucky. A little baby Amy.

Amy Calvin.

Sasha Sorry?

Amy I'm going to call it Calvin. If it's a boy.

Sasha No way!

Amy What?

Sasha We'll both be living with Calvins. What are the chances?

Amy What?

Sasha Calvin's my boof's name.

Amy Wow. Really?

Sasha Yeah. Are you thinking Calvin as in Calvin and Hobbes?

Amy No.

Sasha Like the theologian? Cool. My Calvin's got a superhero's name.

Amy *And then it's like* The Matrix. *Bullet time. She says it first in slow motion.*

Sasha Ccc–aaa–lll–vvv–iii–nnn
Kkk–eee–nnn–nnn–eee–ddd–yyy

Amy *Then fast jump-cuts from all angles, repeating over and over.*

Sasha Calvin –

Calvin Calvin –
Kennedy –
Kennedy –
Kennedy –
Calvin Kennedy – Calvin Kennedy – Calvin Kennedy –

Amy I'm sorry?

Sasha You'll meet him in a minute. He's coming down.

Amy He's coming here? Now? Calvin Kennedy is. Wow . . . Calvin Kennedy.

Sasha Yeah. Calvin Kennedy. Great minds think alike . . .

SCENE EIGHT

Tom *So apparently Sasha made me feel like shit. I realise quite how bad when I notice that I am back at my folks for the weekend. I hardly ever go home. Since the move they've turned my bedroom into a sewing room, but I want to watch TV together as a family and eat home-made soup. I want to be sixteen again. And fortunately that's how my mum treats me.*

(*Tom, his mum and gran are watching TV. As they flick through the channels, they pass on* Tat Raffle, Surgical Glove, Pimp My Dog, Johnny Gay *and* Shark Nazis.)

Mum Are there any nice girls at your work, Tom?

Tom I don't know. I mean. Yes. Of course there are.

Mum And are there any special girls?

Tom They're *all* special, Mum.

Mum You're not seeing anyone just now, though?

Tom No.

Gran You're no queer, are you, son?

Mum MOTHER!
You're not, are you? Not that we would mind a bit.

Tom No.

Mum No.

Gran He'd be smarter looking.

Tom I was seeing a girl, but we broke up.

Mum Oh I'm sorry. Was she nice?

Tom Yeah – what kind of question is that? Of course she was nice. God.

Mum Why did you break up?

Tom I don't know. The hectic pace of modern life.

Mum Oh I'm sorry, dear.

Tom No, it isn't, I mean . . .
Forget it.

Mum Why don't you go and see Jessie?

Tom I'm fine here.

Mum A boy of your age shouldn't be sitting in with his mum and his gran on a Saturday night.

Tom I'm fine.

Mum You could go for a drink.

Tom I *could* go for a drink but I came home to see you.

Mum You've seen us.

Tom Are you trying to get rid of me?

Mum Of course not, it's lovely to have you here, but we're just going to be watching the TV.

Gran Speak for yourself, I'm expecting my young lover.

Tom I don't mind watching the TV.

Mum Go on.

Tom Honestly – I'm fine.

Mum Go on. You might meet someone.

Tom *I feel like I'm cramping their style, so I arrange to meet Jessie in the Mason's Apron.*

Jessie Sorry I'm late – the wee man didn't want to go to bed.

Tom How is he?

Jessie Brand new. He starts at the school this year.

Tom Wow. How's Rhoda?

Jessie Same as ever.

Tom Good, it's good to see you.

Jessie What's the occasion?

Tom No occasion – just home to see the folks.

Jessie How are they?

Tom Fine.

Jessie You ready for another?

Tom *I end up getting drunk. Back home drunk. Eight pints of lager, a couple of alcopops and several fluorescent-shots-of-indeterminate-provenance drunk.*

There is a small room above the Mason's Apron which they refer to as The Nightclub. It's no Studio 54. I end up dancing with Johnny McCormack's mum and I assume it is at this point that Jessie leaves me to it and goes home to his son Lesley and his wife Fat Rhoda. And his proper grown-up life which he made out of the ingredients handed to him by our shared childhood. And what did I make out of those same ingredients? A fucking mess.

He certainly isn't about when I end up winching Mrs McCormack on the dance floor, and I don't see him when Mrs McCormack slaps my face and he definitely isn't there when I am poleaxed on the street vomiting pink goo all over the pavement and myself.

But Alison Hamilton is. It's like some horrific Health Education for Scotland anti-drinking advert. She appears from nowhere.

Alison Tom?

Tom Where's Jessie?

Alison Tom? Is that you?

Tom Where's Jessie?

Alison? Alison Hammeron?

Alison Hamilton.

Tom Alison Hammeron, is that really you?

Alison Yes – are you alright?

Tom I'm amazing. Amazing.

Alison You don't look –

Tom This is fate. I was just thinking about you.

Alison Can you get up?

Tom I'm fine. Honestly. I'm fine. I'm just a bit – You know. Better out than in.

Alison But maybe better in than all over your jumper.

Tom It's fine. It's just a shit jumper anyway.

(*He attempts to pull his jumper over his head but gets stuck.*)

How are you?

Alison Let me help you up.

Tom Alison Hammeron.

Alison There you go.

Tom It's really brilliant to see you.

Alison Yeah, you too. Are you sure you're okay?

Tom Me? I'm brilliant. Brilliant. What are you doing now? I heard you're a farmer.

Alison I'm a pharmacist.

Tom With all the cows and everything. That's brilliant.

Alison Do you want me to see you home?

Tom Yes.

She walks me up the road . . .

Alison Come on.

Tom *. . . and I tell her I love her, that I've never stopped loving her and that it is our destiny be together.*

I fucking love you, Alison Hammeron.

She tells me she's married.

Alison I'm married.

Tom *So I tell her I'm having a baby.*

I'm having a baby.

Alison Really? That's amazing news. Who with?

Tom With Amy.

Alison Who's Amy?

Tom Just some girl from my work.

Alison Well. That's . . . good news.

Tom But I love you.

Alison Tom – we were sixteen.

Tom But I loved you.

Alison Well – that's us here. Goodnight, Tom.

Tom I really did, though. I really, really loved you.

Alison I know. You made it clear at the time. Goodnight, Tom.

Tom 'Goodnight, Tom'? I loved you and you fucking ruined my life. 'Goodnight, Tom' – that's it?

Alison What?

Tom You fucking ruined my life, Alison. You fucking treated me like shit the whole time and you fucking broke my heart and you ruined my life.

Alison Are you serious?

Tom Uh-huh, I'm serious.

Alison I'm sorry you feel that way. I don't think it's really my problem, though.

Tom No. Of course it's not. Of course not. Not Alison Hamilton's problem, no. It's my problem. It's my problem you caused.

Alison Oh get over yourself, Tom. You're thirty-one.

Tom I'm thirty-one and I still haven't recovered from how you treated me. You're a stone cold bitch, Alison Hamilton.

Alison You've got problems.

Tom You're my problems.

Alison I can't believe I'm having this conversation. Tom – we were kids.

Tom I know. You broke my heart.

Alison That's what happens when you're seventeen, Tom.

Tom You slept with Mr Wood.

Alison No, I didn't.

Tom You did.

Alison No, I didn't! Mr Wood got all the girls from band who were leaving school drunk and he kissed me. And I let him. For about a minute. I tried to tell you before I left but you wouldn't listen.

Tom No, but I forgave you . . .

Alison You slept with Michelle McGill.

Tom I-what-did-I-do-with-who?

Alison You slept with Michelle McGill. Rhoda Cree told me. She phoned me up in Canada just to tell me because she hated me because I was first clarinet and she was second clarinet.

Tom I didn't sleep with Michelle McGill . . .
Oh.

I did though. I had no idea that I did until that very moment but then the memory returned, fully formed and toxic.

Jessie Honestly, mate – you take Michelle – I don't actually mind going with big Rhoda.

Tom Right. Fuck it. I'm going to shag Michelle McGill. I'm going to shag her right up. That'll show fucking Alison Hamilton and fucking Mr Wood and you just fucking watch me. How do I smell?

Jessie Dynamite, mate.

Alison Tom, this shouldn't matter to you now anyway – it's ancient history. You're having a baby.

Tom I'm having a baby . . .

She's right. I'm thirty-one years old. This all happened a life ago. Why does it still matter? What's wrong with me? Suddenly I see with a clear eye who I am. What I have done. Become.

Lisa Boyle Just someone else.

Jenny Cooper I can probably do better.

Laura Ferguson You gives me the creeps.

Catrina Collins He's my stepbrother.

Tom I'm sorry.

Alison Forget it. Now go to bed and sleep it off. You'll feel pretty stupid about all this in the morning.

Tom *And I do.*

SCENE NINE

Amy *So this is Calvin Kennedy. Age thirty-three.*

Calvin I'm a fundraiser. For a charity.

Amy *He's a twonk, isn't he?*

Calvin I spent a lot of my twenties travelling.

Amy *Of course. I barely recognise this Calvin Kennedy as my Calvin Kennedy.*

Calvin I take photographs. I've got this really cool old camera and I develop the pictures myself.

Sasha He's *so* talented.

Amy *Eventually Sasha goes to the toilet.*

Calvin It really is excellent to see you, Amy. Really. I couldn't believe it when I saw you. I mean. I can't believe you're Amy from Sash's work. I've heard about a million stories about you. And I never – I mean. Wow.

Amy Yeah. Wow. I'm blown away. It really is a small world.

Calvin Scotland's small – you should see Asia. Give you a sense of perspective.

Amy . . .

Amy Yes?

Calvin I just know you're going to make a tremendous mother.

Sash told me when you were at the loo. I hope you don't mind. She's just so excited. We're both just delighted for you. Both of us.

Amy Thanks.

Do you still have the tattoo?

Calvin Em. Sort of.

Amy Sort of?

Calvin I em . . . I got it changed.

Amy Of course you did. I understand.

Calvin I'll show you.

(*He lifts up his sleeve. In small letters on his arm the tattoo now reads:*)

Amy 'MANY MAKES A VERY'.

Calvin Many makes a very.

Amy Many makes a very . . .
What does that mean?

Calvin You know. It's about unity. Collective action. Positivity. I try to be engaged with the world – you know?

'Amy MacIlvanney' is hard to change. 'It isn't like Winona.'

Amy Yeah.

Calvin I don't know what I was thinking.

Amy It is a bit inane.

Calvin No. I meant. When I was eighteen. Not . . .

Amy Sorry. I know. That's what I meant. Sorry.

It's a lot smaller than I remembered.

Calvin It didn't feel small when I was getting it.

Amy You know – I always thought it was on your back.

Calvin No. No, it wasn't. No.

Amy God. Isn't memory funny?

I don't stand up and scream at him that he's ruined my life, that he's not who he's meant to be, that he's just shit.
I don't cry or laugh or display any emotions on the outside. Even though my heart is breaking.

Craig Bryson I got you something.

Gary Hay I made you a quiche.

Cammy Bell They're plastic. So they'll last for ever.

Manuel Pascali For you, bella Amy.

Conor Sammon I got you a vibrating dildo.

Amy *I feel sick. Nothing's perfect. Nothing's terrible. There's just people trying. Fucking trying.*

I try and remember him like before and I can't. He's no longer played by a young Christian Slater. Now it's just this gonky cunt leering at me from inside every memory.

Sasha Is he showing you his tat? 'Many makes a very'. Very cool, huh?

Amy *What am I doing? I'm having a baby. Alone. Because I'm lonely and I don't want cats. This is fucking ridiculous. I should be put on a register.*

I need to go.

Sasha Oh, okay. See you at work tomorrow.

Calvin Bye, Amy. It was really great seeing you again.

Amy Yeah. Great.

I was going to call it Calvin.
I don't cancel the appointment at the place. I have tomorrow booked as annual leave and I'm going to finish this. I wish I could go there right now.
Drop in. Drive through. I want to speak to Tom – tell him I'm sorry I've been a psycho. I pull out my phone, it's been on silent, sixty-three missed calls.

SCENE TEN

Tom I'm sorry.

Amy It's okay.

Tom Really though. About it all. I didn't mean . . . I haven't . . . I'm sorry.
How have you been?

Amy I don't know – fine.

Tom Are you . . . have you . . .

Amy Yes?

Tom Have you already had the – Em. Have you been for the – Eh. The –

Amy Not yet. I see the T2000 tomorrow.

Tom The T2000?

Amy The Terminator.

Tom Right, right.
So you're still . . . I mean. You are actually still . . .

Amy Pregnant. Just.

Tom Don't.

Amy What?

Tom Em. Don't have it terminated. Don't. I'm sorry. My timing is shit. I know. I know. But don't. I've been stupid, weak, selfish. I've been a cunt. I know. But don't have an abortion. I was wrong. I've been thinking . . .

Amy Don't . . .

Tom You don't need to make a decision now –

Amy I've made the decision, Tom –

Tom I mean, I know I'm just piling this on you. And I know I'm so fucking late and that I should have been better at the time, I realise that, Amy, I do, but better late than never, you know? I mean –

Amy Can I speak?

Tom Uh-huh. Sure. Sorry.

Amy FUCK YOU, TOM. You. Are. Too. Late.

Tom I'm not, though. I know there's something, Amy. I know there's something I can say . . .

Amy There isn't. There really isn't.

Tom I've had my head up my arse. I've been living in a dream world, Amy. In a bubble.

Amy This whole thing has been a complete disaster from day one. We've both been . . .
Let's just cut our losses. Do the right thing.

Tom No. Please, Amy. Please.

Amy Don't.

Tom Please, just . . .

Amy Don't.

Tom Please.

Amy The decision's made. It isn't your decision. You know. Really. This . . . is sweet and everything but . . . I'm not . . . I'm not . . . I'm not ready, Tom.

Tom But we can do this. We can. I know it's not ideal, but . . .

Amy No. No, Tom. We can't. Stop. 'Not ideal', Jesus. Stop it. You can't turn shit into gold. A baby can't make this right.

Tom You need time to think about it.

Amy Christ, I have been. I have been thinking about it. All I do is think about it.

Tom *We talk.*

Amy *We talk properly for what seems like maybe it's the first time.*

Tom *But she doesn't change her mind.*

Amy *I don't change my mind.*

Tom *And I don't blame her.*

Amy *Too little too late.*

And then the next day the receptionist says –

Receptionist Hi, can I help you?

Tom *And Amy says –*

Amy Hi. I've got an appointment.

And the receptionist says –

Receptionist What's your name?

Amy *And I say –*

MacIlvanney.

And she says –

Receptionist Amy? I've got you. Now there's a bit of paperwork, I'm afraid. Here. Can you fill in these for me, please?

Amy Thanks.

And he says –

Tom Are you okay?

And she says –

Amy I'm fine.

And he says –

Tom Well. This is okay, isn't it?

Amy *I say –*

Yes.

Even though it isn't. It's horrible. It's like a dentist's without the magazines. And there's a young girl of about sixteen who looks like she's going to cry or be sick or something.

Then he says –

Tom I mean, it's institutional and sterile and everything, but it's one of those ones where at least they've tried, you know?

And she can see me trying too and so she tries and says –

Amy Yes.

Tom *And we're both trying. It's awful.*

Amy *Unfamiliar.*

Tom *Polite. But I keep talking. The words just fall out my open mouth. Like they sometimes do. And the words that fall out are always the worst words.*

Amy Shut up.

I say. Eventually. But I'm happy he's here.

Tom *And I'm glad she stopped me. I say –*

Sorry. I'm sorry. Sorry.

Amy *I don't know why, where it comes from, it's not like I was even thinking about it, my mind is pretty occupied with . . . all . . . this, but I suddenly say –*

What are you doing on September the 20th?

Tom I don't know – why?

Amy My mum is getting married. Would you want to . . . Forget it. It doesn't matter just now.

Tom No, no. I'd like to come. Is that? Are you asking me?

Amy Yeah. It'll be shit. Most likely. Just, you know . . .

Tom No, no, seriously – yes.

Amy Okay.

Tom *and* **Amy** (*together*) *And then the receptionist says –*

Receptionist Amy? We're ready for you now.

Amy *And he says –*

Tom I'll wait here for you.

Amy You don't have to.

Tom I'll wait for you.

And I wait for her.

Amy *And he waits for me.*

The End.